W9-AVJ-773

The Colony of Massachusetts

A Primary Source History

Jake Miller

The Rosen Publishing Group's
PowerKids Press™
New York

Published in 2006 by The Rosen Publishing Group, Inc.
29 East 21st Street, New York, NY 10010

First Edition

Editor: Jennifer Way
Book Design: Ginny Chu

Photo Credits: Cover, p. 12 Courtesy of Pilgrim Hall Museum, Plymouth, Massachusetts; p. 4 © Bettmann/Corbis; p. 4 (inset) Image Select / Art Resource, NY; p. 6 Private Collection/Bridgeman Art Library; p. 6 (inset) akg-images; p. 8 © Burstein Collection/Corbis; p. 8 (inset) Courtesy of the State Library of Massachusetts; pp. 10, 16 Library of Congress Geography and Map Division; p. 10 (inset) Courtesy of Massachusetts Archives; pp. 11, 16 (inset), 18 (inset) Library of Congress Prints and Photographs Division; p. 12 (inset) © Getty Images; p. 14 The Mariners' Museum, Newport News, VA; p. 14 (inset) Mary Evans Picture Library; p. 18 New York Public Library / Art Resource, NY; p. 20 © North Wind Picture Archives; p. 20 (inset) Courtesy U.S. Naval Historical Center.

Library of Congress Cataloging-in-Publication Data

Miller, Jake, 1969–
   The colony of Massachusetts : a primary source history / Jake Miller. — 1st ed.
      p. cm. — (The primary source library of the thirteen colonies and the Lost Colony)
   Includes bibliographical references (p.   ) and index.
   ISBN 1-4042-3028-9 (library binding)
   1. Massachusetts—History—Colonial period, ca. 1600–1775—Juvenile literature. 2. Massachusetts—History—1775–1865—Juvenile literature.   I. Title. II. Series.
F67.M65 2006
974.4'02—dc22

2004019477

Manufactured in the United States of America

Contents

In 1497, John Cabot went to Newfoundland, which is now part of Canada. In 1498, he became the first European to see the coast of Massachusetts, where he may have seen Algonquin camps similar to the one in the painting above. Inset: Cabot was looking for a fast route to Asia. No one knew what lands or oceans lay between Europe and Asia, because much of the world had not yet been mapped.

Early Explorers

People have lived in North America for thousands of years. The first people to settle on the land that became Massachusetts were the **ancestors** of the **Algonquin** Native Americans. They came to Massachusetts almost 10,000 years ago. In the 1400s, European kings began to send **explorers** to search for new lands. They were looking for places to find gold, spices, and other goods. They were also looking for faster and safer trade routes to Asia.

John Cabot made the first recorded European journey to Massachusetts in 1498. Many years passed before Europeans settled there. In 1606, James I, king of England, gave the Plymouth Company a **charter** to settle the eastern coast of North America. This area was later named New England.

This map of the colony was created in the seventeenth century. Inset: The Mayflower was supposed to land farther south, in Virginia. After a storm at sea blew the Pilgrims off course, they landed on Cape Cod, a few hundred miles (km) to the north. They established the Plymouth Colony nearby.

Accidental Settlers

The Plymouth Company had a hard time finding people who wanted to settle in New England. A religious group known as the **Pilgrims** became the first successful English settlers in New England. This group had been moving across Europe in search of a place where they could practice their beliefs freely. They lived in England in a time when the king wanted everyone to follow the Church of England. The Pilgrims decided to seek freedom in the new land.

On a ship called the *Mayflower*, 102 Pilgrims sailed for Virginia, in North America, in 1620. They landed on what is now known as Cape Cod, Massachusetts. They decided to settle in a nearby place that they named Plymouth.

From the Mayflower Compact

"Having undertaken…a voyage to plant the first colony in the northern parts of Virginia; do by these presents, solemnly and mutually in the Presence of God and one of another, covenant and combine ourselves together into a civil Body Politick, for our better Ordering and Preservation . . ."

The Mayflower Compact was written before the Pilgrims landed in North America. Above: The signers of the Compact agree to work together to govern themselves. They believe that this is important for order and for their new colony to succeed.

The first Thanksgiving in North America was celebrated in 1621. The Wampanoag brought venison, or deer meat, to the feast. The feast lasted for several days and included games and races. Thanksgiving became an official national holiday in 1867. Inset: This is Governor William Bradford's copy of the Mayflower Compact.

The First Colony in Massachusetts

The Pilgrims did not settle where they had received their charter, so they made an agreement about how they would govern themselves. This was called the Mayflower Compact. This document was an important step in building the kind of government that the United States has today.

When the Pilgrims landed, they were not prepared for the rough conditions. In their first winter in Massachusetts, half of the Pilgrims died from hunger and sickness. Next spring the local Wampanoag and Narraganset Native Americans helped the colonists learn to plant beans and corn, dig clams, and catch fish. That fall, when the crops were picked, the Pilgrims and the Native Americans had a feast together. That feast became known as the first Thanksgiving.

9

This eighteenth-century map shows Boston, Massachusetts. The town was named for Boston in England, the town from which many of the colony's original settlers came. Inset: The first Massachusetts Bay Colony seal was created in 1629. The seal was used until 1686, and again from 1689 until 1692.

The Colony Grows

In 1629, King Charles I granted a charter to the Massachusetts Bay Colony. The name "Massachusetts" came from the name of one of the Native American groups that lived there.

From 1630 to 1640, more than 14,000 people came to the colony. Some people came looking for religious freedom. Others came because they wanted to own land. Merchants **invested** in colonies and came themselves to make money. Many of these people started new towns, such as Boston, which was founded in 1630. The Pilgrims' settlement in Plymouth became part of this new colony in 1641.

Education was important to the Puritans. The oldest public school in America is in Boston. It is called Boston Latin School. It opened in Boston in 1635 and is still open today.

Harvard University, shown above, is the oldest college in America. It opened in Cambridge, Massachusetts, in 1636. Its original purpose was to train ministers. Today it is a world-famous university.

Wampanoag leader Metacomet wanted to prevent settlers from moving onto Wampanoag lands. The two groups had once been able to settle their differences peacefully, such as by signing treaties, shown above. Inset: Metacomet was called King Philip by the colonists. About 600 settlers and 3,000 Native Americans were killed in King Philip's War.

Trouble in Massachusetts

As the Massachusetts Colony began to grow, the colonists faced many problems. The cold winters made farming hard. There were also many disagreements about land. The Native Americans were willing to share their land with the colonists, but the colonists wanted to own the land.

The colonists thought they owned the land once they made an agreement with the Native Americans to use it. When the Native Americans realized they were losing their land, they began fighting to keep it. One example of this was King Philip's War, which lasted from 1675 until 1676 and was fought in Massachusetts.

King Philip's War

At first the Native Americans won many battles in King Philip's War, but as more colonists moved to Massachusetts, the Native Americans were driven onto smaller pieces of land. Without use of the land, they could not hunt or farm anymore and had to go to work for the English doing labor on their farms.

The plentiful lumber in the Massachusetts Colony led to a successful shipbuilding trade, as shown in the above painting. These ships were used by fishermen and also were sold to other countries. Inset: Massachusetts merchants began to trade with colonies in the Caribbean that produced sugar on large farms called plantations.

Many Roads to Success

Despite early hardships with farming and with their Native American neighbors, the Massachusetts colonists were becoming successful by the late 1600s. For example, the colonists began to produce enough extra beef and butter to sell to the British colonies in the Caribbean. The colonists there grew sugar on large farms called plantations. They traded this sugar with colonies like Massachusetts for the other foods and supplies they needed.

In the 1640s, the fishing trade began to grow in Massachusetts. There were a lot of fish in the waters off the coast. The colonists sold fish to the Spanish and the Portuguese and to the English colonies in the West Indies. In 1641, New England fishing boats caught 600,000 pounds (272,155 kg) of fish. By 1675, they caught 6 million pounds (2.7 million kg) per year.

This map shows the Massachusetts Colony as it looked in the mid-1700s. The towns of Boston, Lexington, and Charlestown are circled in yellow. Inset: King George III was king of Great Britain and Ireland from 1760 until 1820.

The King Tries to Take Control

By the 1700s, Britain controlled 13 colonies in North America, including Massachusetts. During the **French and Indian War**, which lasted from 1754 to 1763, Britain spent a lot of money to protect its American colonies. George III, the king at the time, thought that the colonies should pay for the cost of the war.

King George III and **Parliament** created many new taxes for the colonists to pay. In Britain the landowning men got to elect **representatives** to decide how much tax they would pay. The colonists did not have representation in Parliament, so they felt that they should not be taxed. In 1764, the king created the Sugar Act. The colonists stopped buying sugar to fight the unfair tax. In 1768, the king sent an army to America to force the colonists to obey the new laws.

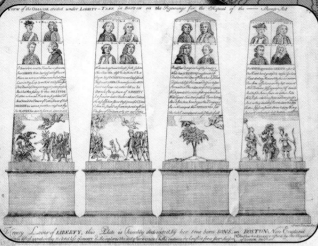

From the Sons of Liberty Column

"To every lover of liberty, this plate is humbly dedicated by her true born sons, in Boston New England: 1. America in distress apprehending the total loss of liberty 2: She implores the aid of her Patrons 3. She endures the Conflict for a short season 4. And has her Liberty restored by the Royal hand of George the Third."

The above passage is taken from the bottom of the picture, which explains the drawings that show the Sons of Liberty's role in ending the Stamp Act. This column was made to honor them. First the colony's freedom is hurt by the act. Next the colony asks the Sons for help. The colony suffers for a short while before the unfair tax ends, returning the colony to liberty.

British warships block Boston Harbor under the Boston Port Bill, one of the four Intolerable Acts, in this print by Paul Revere from around 1774 . Inset: Paul Revere made this plan for a column, or post, which honored the Sons of Liberty and the end of an unfair tax called the Stamp Act. The column was made from oiled paper and was lit from the inside by lamps.

The Massachusetts Colonists Fight Back

The new taxes made the colonists angry. Some men in Boston formed a group called the Sons of Liberty. These men joined to **protest** the unfair laws.

On March 5, 1770, a group of British soldiers got into a fight with a small group of colonists, killing five people. When news of this event spread, it became known as the Boston Massacre.

Another famous protest was called the Boston Tea Party. To protest a tea tax, the Sons of Liberty stormed three ships on December 16, 1773. They threw 342 cases of tea into Boston Harbor. Parliament answered the protest by passing four laws, called the **Coercive Acts**, in 1774.

Colonists called the Coercive Acts the Intolerable Acts. The Boston Port Bill closed the city's harbor. The Massachusetts Government Act reduced the power of colonial government. The Administration of Justice Act limited the power of colonial courts. The Quartering Act said colonists had to house British soldiers. The laws angered the colonists and made them want to fight the British even more.

The first shot fired in the Battle of Lexington and Concord was later called the "shot heard 'round the world." The painting above is a re-creation of the battle. Inset: The misnamed Battle of Bunker Hill took place in Charlestown. The British report of the battle said the fighting had taken place on Bunker Hill, when most of the battle had taken place on nearby Breed's Hill.

Fighting the War

After the Coercive Acts were passed, leaders from each colony met in Philadelphia, Pennsylvania, on September 5, 1774. They talked about ways to protest Great Britain's actions. This was called the **Continental Congress**.

The first battle of the **American Revolution** took place in Massachusetts. On April 19, 1775, the Battle of Lexington and Concord occurred.

A few months later, on June 17, 1775, a small group of colonial soldiers fought against a large group of British soldiers in the Battle of Bunker Hill in Boston. The colonists lost the battle, but they showed that they could fight bravely.

Declaration of Independence

The Second Continental Congress met in May 1775 and again in July 1776. At the July 1776 meeting, the leaders announced their independence from England. John Hancock, one of the representatives from Massachusetts, signed the Declaration of Independence in big letters, so King George could read it without his eyeglasses.

Massachusetts Becomes a State

In October 1780, Massachusetts' **constitution** was adopted. The constitution explained the rights and responsibilities of the people of Massachusetts. Massachusetts was now a state that had the right to make its own laws and to decide its own taxes. The other 12 states made constitutions, too. The states worked together under a loose set of laws called the Articles of Confederation.

After the war ended in 1783, the leaders of the states tried to work together as a country under the articles. The articles gave the individual states more power than the federal government. This made it difficult for the states to work together as a nation. In 1787, representatives met to write a constitution for the nation. On February 6, 1788, Massachusetts approved the Constitution and became the sixth state in the United States.

Glossary

Algonquin (al-GAHN-kwin) Referring to Native Americans who lived in eastern North America.

American Revolution (uh-MER-uh-ken reh-vuh-LOO-shun) Battles that soldiers from the colonies fought against Britain for freedom, from 1775 to 1783.

ancestors (AN-ses-terz) Relatives who lived long ago.

charter (CHAR-tur) An official agreement giving someone permission to do something.

Coercive Acts (koh-ER-siv AKTS) The laws that the British government passed after the Boston Tea Party. The colonists called them the Intolerable Acts.

constitution (kon-stih-TOO-shun) The basic rules by which a country or a state is governed.

Continental Congress (kon-tin-NEN-tul KON-gres) A group, made up of a few people from every colony, that made decisions for the colonies.

explorers (ek-SPLOR-urz) People who travel and look for new land.

French and Indian War (FRENCH AND IN-dee-in WOR) The battles fought between 1754 and 1763 by England, France, and Native Americans for control of North America.

invested (in-VEST-id) To have put money into something, such as a company, in the hope of getting more money later on.

Parliament (PAR-lih-mint) The group in England that makes the country's laws.

Pilgrims (PIL-grumz) The people who sailed on the *Mayflower* in 1620 from England to America in search of freedom to practice their own beliefs.

protest (PROH-test) To act out in disagreement.

representatives (reh-prih-ZEN-tuh-tivz) People chosen to speak for others.

Index

Primary Sources

Page 6. *Map of Plymouth, Massachusetts.* Ink on paper, 17th century, English School, Private Collection. **Page 8. Inset.** William Bradford's copy of the Mayflower Compact, from *History of Plimoth Plantation.* Circa 1630, The State Library of Massachusetts/Special Collections Department. **Page 10.** *Plan de la ville et du port de Boston; capitale de la Nouvelle Angleterre.* Hand-colored print, circa 1764, Jacques Nicolas Bellin. **Inset.** The first seal of the Massachusetts Bay Colony. 1629, Massachusetts Public Records Division, Secretary of the Commonwealth of Massachusetts. **Page 11.** *A Westerly view of the colledges [sic] in Cambridge, New England.* Circa 1900 after 18th century original, Josh Chadwick, after Paul Revere, Library of Congress Prints and Photographs Division. **Page 16.** A new and accurate map of the colony of Massachusetts Bay in North America, from a late source. Etching with watercolor, 1780, J. Hinton, Library of Congress, Geography and Map Division. **Inset.** *King George III.* Engraving, circa 1802, Robert Hartley Cromek, Library of Congress. **Page 18.** *A Southeast view of the Great town of Boston in New England in America.* Colored engraving, circa 18th century, William Burgis, engraved by John Carwitham, Miriam and Ira D. Wallach Division, New York Public Library. **Inset.** *A view of the obelisk erected under Liberty-tree in Boston on the rejoicings for the repeal of the — Stamp Act 1766.* Paul Revere, Library of Congress and appeared in *Harper's Weekly* in 1766. **Page 20. Inset.** View of the attack on Bunker's Hill, with the burning of Charles Town, June 17, 1775. Etching, circa 1783, drawn by Mr. Millar, engraved by John Lodge, courtesy, U.S. Naval Historical Center.

Web Sites

Due to the changing nature of Internet links, PowerKids Press has developed an online list of Web sites related to the subject of this book. This site is updated regularly. Please use this link to access the list:
www.powerkidslinks.com/pstclc/massachus/